a ^Smart girl's guide to
sticky
situations

how to tackle tricky, icky
problems and tough times

from the editors of American Girl
illustrated by Bonnie Timmons

American★Girl ®

Published by Pleasant Company Publications
Copyright © 2002, 2005 by American Girl, LLC
All rights reserved. No part of this book may be used or reproduced in any manner whatsoever without written
permission except in the case of brief quotations embodied in critical articles and reviews.

Questions or comments? Call 1-800-845-0005, visit our Web site at **americangirl.com**,
or write Customer Service, American Girl, 8400 Fairway Place, Middleton, WI 53562-0497.

Printed in China.
07 08 09 10 C&C 10 9 8 7 6 5

American Girl™ and its associated logos are trademarks of American Girl, LLC.
Editorial Development: Nancy Holyoke, Michelle Watkins, Therese Maring
Art Direction and Design: Chris David
Production: Kendra Schluter, Mindy Rappe, Jeannette Bailey, Judith Lary
Illustrations: Bonnie Timmons

Information, suggestions, and advice in this book are provided as a resource to the reader based on research
available at the time of publication. This book is not intended to replace the opinion or recommendations of
any expert or professional on any subject matter discussed. The reader should address her individual questions
or concerns to her parents, teachers, counselors, physician, and other professionals and experts. The names
of individuals involved have been changed to preserve their privacy.

Cataloging-in-Publication Data available from Library of Congress

Special thanks to:

American Red Cross, Badger Chapter

American School Counselor Association

California Surf Lifesaving Association

Winky Cherry, *My First Sewing Book*

Chicago Inline Skate School, IL

Children's Theater Association, Inc.

City of Madison Fire Department, WI

The Empower Program

Federal Emergency Management Association
for Kids

John Holyoke, teaching artist, New York City
public schools

Hunterdon County Parks Department, NJ

International Fabricare Institute

International Inline Skating Association

Madison Dressage and Training Center, WI

Madison Police Department, WI

Dr. Patricia McConnell, zoologist, Dog's
Best Friend

Dr. Cynthia Mehta, dermatologist

National Center for Missing and Exploited
Children

National Fire Protection Agency

National Institutes of Health

National Oceanic and Atmospheric
Administration

Oriental Rug Cleaning Company

Palm Beach County Beach Patrol, FL

Dr. Megeen Parker, M.D.

Phil Pelliteri, University of Wisconsin
Entomology Department

Playtex Apparel, Inc.

Dr. Dave Riley, child development specialist

Dr. Judy Van Raalte, sports psychologist

www.saferchild.org

Dear Reader,

Every now and then you're going to find yourself in a bad situation. All girls do. All people do. The situation may be awkward. It may be embarrassing. It may be scary. It may simply make you unhappy. What do you do?

This book tries to answer that question. It gives tips and advice on surviving all sorts of sticky situations that a girl might face in daily life. But it also gives you a few big ideas about ways to tackle problems—strategies that you can use on any problem, not just the ones in this book.

You can't control the world. But you can control how you deal with it. You can learn. You can be smart. You can trust your confidence and your common sense. You can take charge of your own tough situations. And that's what we hope you'll have learned when you close this book.

Your friends at American Girl

 # contents

quick thinking 7

solving the impossible 19

contents (cont.)

quick thinking

Quick thinking requires trusting yourself and knowing what's important (and what isn't).

if your friend tells the whole school which boy you like

1. People will take their cue from you. If you act like this is a major crisis, other kids will play it up until it is. So **stay calm.** When a group comes around the corner ready to give you grief, pretend they're talking in ancient Greek. Give them a look that says, "What on earth are you talking about and why are you getting so excited?" It will slow them down, at the very least.

2. If they keep needling you, **act bored.** Say, "Hey, if you want to make a big fuss about nothing, go ahead."

3. Has the boy himself heard the news? If so, everyone will be watching to see you cringe when he goes by. Don't do it. **Be brave** and talk to him. Say,

Sorry my friend started this stupid rumor. It's a big pain.

Lisa
likes
Patrick

4. Of course, you might also ask yourself if this is really **all bad.** If the boy likes you too, maybe you'll start out talking about the silly rumor and end up sitting together at lunch.

5. If you **never intended** this crush to go further than daydreams—if, say, this boy has already got a girlfriend or is three years older than you—then you may want to cover your tracks. Say: "He seems nice, but I hardly know the guy." You can vary that with: "I heard that rumor, too. It's made *my* day pretty exciting." Tell people that you were talking with your friend about boys you liked—not boys you *liked.*

Vary these strategies depending on the situation. One way or another, what you're saying to the teasers is that they can pester you all they want, but you're not going to get upset. And it's a way of telling yourself that, too.

if you forget your lines onstage

1. **Keep doing** whatever your character is doing. That is, if your character is drumming her fingers on a desk looking bored, keep drumming your fingers and looking bored while you think.

2. Ask yourself **what happens next** in the story. Can you remember what other people onstage usually do next? Sometimes remembering these things will help you remember your line.

3. If you know the gist of what your character is supposed to say but can't remember the specific words, **make something up.** In other words, "Come in" will work if you are blanking on the line "Enter if you dare, Mr. President."

4. Your fellow actors may realize you're stuck and go on without you. If so, think of them as **members of your team.** They're going to serve the ball back to you, and you can pick up your lines and get back in the game.

5. If you're onstage and someone else forgets a line, **give her a moment** to remember. Whispering the line or giving her one of those "IT'S YOUR LINE!" looks isn't going to help. Chances are, the line is on the tip of her tongue, and scaring her with panicked looks is only going to drive it away.

disaster blaSter

While you're still rehearsing, spend time thinking about why your character does what she does in different scenes. What's she feeling? What does she want? The more you understand your character, the easier it will be for you to remember lines (and to fake it when you don't).

if your zipper breaks

1. **Cover yourself** with anything you can grab—a sweater, a book, a backpack, your cat Louise. Then find a private place to inspect the damage.

2. Close the gap with a **safety pin** or two.

3. Get a **big shirt**—borrow one if you have to. It will hide the problem till you can get home and change.

4. When you waltz back into public view, **don't act worried.** Don't fiddle with the shirt. Don't touch the zipper. It will only draw attention to the last place you want it to go.

disaster blaSter

Is the problem a few broken teeth at the bottom of the zipper? If so, it can be fixed by using a needle and thread to make a dozen stitches an inch above the trouble spot. The zipper will be shorter, but it will still work.

if the popcorn in the microwave catches fire

1. If you see smoke leaking out around the door of your microwave, turn the oven **off** by hitting the stop button, and unplug the unit. This will stop the fan, which is the first step in containing the smoke and suffocating any fire.

2. Don't open the door. That door is keeping the smoke and flames away from you and the rest of the kitchen, and it's cutting off air that could feed flames.

3. Get an **adult.** If your parents aren't home, call a trusted friend or neighbor. She can help judge the situation. Usually microwave fires go out on their own, but if there's any doubt, you'll need to call the fire department.

4. Don't disconnect the smoke alarm, however annoying it is. (And it will be annoying—VERY.) Instead, open a window and air the place out.

5. When the oven door is **cool** enough that you can touch it, open the door and remove the bag. Should the adult still be there? Yep.

6. Run **water** over the bag of popcorn before you throw it away. It's a good way to be sure there's nothing left that could spark a fire in the trash.

7. Take out the garbage: it's going to **smell.**

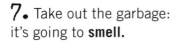

disaster blaSter

Always stay in the kitchen when you're cooking microwave popcorn, so that if it begins to burn, you can smell it. And if it has ever occurred to you to put regular popcorn in a brown paper bag and nuke that—forget it. Not all bags are created equal, and a fire might well result.

if you

can't stop on inline skates

1. Head for some **grass**—or anything else that's softer than pavement.

2. Get low. **Bend your knees** and sink to a crouch. Put your hands on your knees if it helps steady you.

3. Put one skate in front of the other to **widen your base** of support.

4. Keep your weight on your **back skate** as you skate or step onto the grass.

5. Running **a few steps** on the grass will help you stay standing.

6. If you know you're going to fall, go down **knees first.** (Better have those pads on.) Try not to take the full force of the fall on your hands.

disaster blaSter

There are two effective ways of stopping. Learn them before you slip on those skates. Take a lesson if you can.

brake stop

If your skate has a heel brake, use it. Keep your knees bent and your arms straight out ahead. Slide your brake foot in front of your other foot, and then, with both knees bent, lift the toe till you feel the brake make contact with the ground. Sink down, bending your knees even more, to put pressure on the brake. Hold that position until you stop.

T-stop

Once again, start by bending your knees and sliding one foot in front of the other. Put your weight on your forward foot. Turn your back foot so that together your feet make a T. Drag the inside edges of the wheels on your back skate till it slows you down.

- Look before you skate. Walk or bike the route before you skate it. Sometimes a hill looks a lot different when you're going down it than it did when you were standing at the top.

- Should you wear the gear? Of course. But don't imagine that pads and helmets protect you from everything. If you can't handle a bump, stop for a car, or swerve for a squirrel, you're going too fast. Slow down while you still have the chance.

if a tampon falls out of your backpack

1. Pick it up—**quick.** Try not to look panicked. Put it back. Say, "Well, that was embarrassing."

2. Change the subject. That tampon thing is done, past, over, **finished.** You're moving on. Anyone who wants to embarrass you by laughing for the next half hour can do it without your help.

disaster bla**S**ter

Don't let those tampons float around loose in your backpack. Zip them up in a pouch or an old eyeglass case.

solving the impossible

Use your ingenuity. Creative thinking solves problems.

if you're dressed all wrong

1. Feel too fancy? **Subtract** some of the glitz. Take off the velvet headband. Shake out your hair. Stick your bracelets in your pocket. Maybe you can put the shoes in a corner and cover the satiny blouse with your sweater.

If you're so overdressed that you can't participate in party activities without wrecking your clothes, ask your hostess if you can **borrow** something else.

2. Not fancy enough? This is harder. **Tuck in** your shirt. Comb your hair. Again, see if there is something you can do without—the torn sweatshirt, the gruddy sneakers. Maybe another guest or your hostess has a big shirt or a nicer sweater you can borrow.

Most important: Carry yourself as if you're dressed to the nines. Use your **best manners.** Poise and politeness can go a long way toward making up for a snag in the wardrobe.

disaster blaSter

It never hurts to make a phone call before an event
to see what other people are wearing.

if you hate your new haircut

Let's not overdo it.

1. Sometimes the difference between a darling 'do and disaster lies in the **styling.** Experiment. Get some gel and a blow-dryer and see how things look:

windswept

poofy

swirly

Get your friends or your big sister to help. See what you can come up with.

2. Get creative with your **barrettes.**

3. Headbands. Like barrettes, they give you a way to rearrange your hair and focus attention somewhere else.

4. Hats O.K., it's a little desperate. But there are some very **cute hats** out there, not to mention your favorite baseball cap. Wear one for a week or two, and when you take it off you may find your hair is looking better than you thought. The truth is, lots of bad haircuts mysteriously get better all by themselves in the first few days.

5. Still unhappy? Sometimes the stylist will fix a haircut for free. Or you can hit the piggy bank and **get another haircut.**

disaster blaSter

Look through a few magazines before you go to the salon. Get some pictures of cuts you like. It will make communicating with your stylist a lot easier.

if your teacher hates you

1. What seems to **irritate** her most? The times you and your friend talk in class? Your handwriting? Even if you think she's coming down on you unfairly, try cleaning up your act. Talk a little less. Take more care with your cursive. More effort on your end may be all it takes to soften her up.

2. Talk to your **friends outside class.** Do they think she dislikes you? If they don't see the problem, maybe it's not there.

3. Do your friends think she dislikes them, too? Maybe she's just all-round **crabby.** It's not pleasant, but at least it isn't personal.

4. Is there a parent/teacher conference coming up? Maybe your **mom or dad** can find out what's bugging her. Or maybe she'll tell them that you're a delight to have in class, and you can relax.

5. When all else fails, just **do the work.** Be polite. Don't worry about her. You're getting a lesson in working with a difficult person. Luckily, she won't be your teacher forever.

if your best friend is moving to Australia

(or somewhere else far away)

1. Set a time to meet **online** every week and send instant messages. Send e-mails, too. Is it the same as having your friend sitting at the next desk? No. But it will keep you in touch.

2. Don't forget the **U.S. mail.** Send photos of the soccer match, confetti from the party, a package of her favorite gum. Trade your favorite books and CDs. It'll be fun to think up things to send and exciting when a package turns up in your own mailbox.

3. Use the phone. **Call** on her birthday. Check in on the first day of school.

4. Be a good **listener.** Your friend knows all about your world. You don't know anything about her new one. Ask questions. Learn the names. Take an interest. She'll appreciate it more than you can know.

5. Expect **change.** A year from now, you will each have new friends that you hang out with at the pool and sit by at lunch. But keep the faith with this old friend, too, and the relationship will keep growing in its own way. It could even end up being the most lasting friendship of all.

if you get a pimple on the big day

1. You want to push and squeeze that pimple. **Don't do it.** Messing with pimples leads to infection and scarring. It also often makes the spot look redder and ickier than it did before.

2. Go to your local drugstore and select **a simple concealer** and a light, colorless powder. Ask your mom or sister to come along to help.

3. As you're getting dressed for your big event, put a tiny dab of concealer on the pimple. Wait for it to dry. Then apply the powder. **Go light.** Again, getting help from someone who's got experience with makeup will be a big help.

4. So you're at your event. Your hand wants to touch that spot to make sure things are O.K. But (is there an echo in here?) **don't.** Because (a) that's going to take off your makeup. And (b) it will just call attention to a little bump that nobody is thinking about but you. Leave it alone. Have fun.

saving face

A brave front can help take
the sting out of humiliation.

if your sister reads your diary

1. **Don't yell** or scream or cry. It will make her think she's got the goods on you.

2. Tell her **what you think** of what she did. Keep your head, but let her know you're angry.

3. Keep the focus on her. Don't get drawn into a discussion of what she read. Insist on **your privacy.** Say, "It's private. I'm not going to talk to you about it."

4. Don't respond to **taunts or blackmail.** If your sister says she's going to tell your secrets unless you do this or that, tell her no deal. In this—as in anything—don't give someone else the power to control what you do.

disaster bl**aS**ter

Don't keep your diary on your desk or lying open on the bed. It's asking for trouble. A special hiding spot is what's called for:

In the pocket of the robe you never wear

Inside your old sweatpants at the back of a bureau drawer

Behind the other books on your bookcase

Don't leave the room without putting it away. If it's not in your hands, it should be in its place.

if you throw up at school

1. Don't worry about the mess. Take care of yourself. Splash water on your face in the bathroom. Rinse out your mouth. Clean up and go to the nurse's office. You can worry about your embarrassment **tomorrow.**

2. When tomorrow comes—hey, throwing up was **yesterday.** Push your embarrassment out of your head.

3. Anyway, it's not as if you had a choice. And every kid in your class has thrown up at some point in his life. It's gross but **natural.** So if some bozo comes up and says,

Boy, that stank! look him in the eye and say, Yeah, but it felt even worse.

if you fall down the stairs in front of four million people *(more or less)*

1. Arrange your clothes. **Check** for damage. Don't try to stand up right away.

2. Thank the people who help you gather up your stuff. Don't **rush** as you put it back together. You don't want to drop it all again six feet away.

3. Crack a **joke.**

4. Stand up and walk away. Carefully.

if you're having your period and get blood on your clothes

1. Are you wearing two layers on top? If so, take off your jacket or top shirt and tie it around your waist so **it will hide your backside** when you stand up. If you don't have a sweater or sweatshirt to spare, see if a friend does.

2. If you can, **wait** till the bell rings. Stay in your seat while the kids around you leave theirs.

3. Flag down a **friend.** Ask her to get you a tissue or a paper towel. Use it to wipe any blood off the chair as you stand up. Ask the friend to walk close behind you as you go to a restroom.

4. Once you're in the restroom, send your friend to the office to talk to the nurse. Often a nurse will have a **change of clothes** available for a crisis like this. If not, she can call your parents or figure out some other way to help.

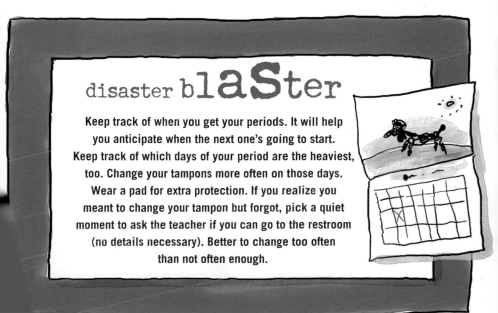

disaster blaSter

Keep track of when you get your periods. It will help you anticipate when the next one's going to start. Keep track of which days of your period are the heaviest, too. Change your tampons more often on those days. Wear a pad for extra protection. If you realize you meant to change your tampon but forgot, pick a quiet moment to ask the teacher if you can go to the restroom (no details necessary). Better to change too often than not often enough.

if your friend's brother sees you naked

1. If you were changing clothes and this boy got a glimpse of you as he passed by the open door, he didn't see a whole lot. A person just doesn't take in much in a **glance.** Tell yourself that. Again and again and again.

2. Shut the door.

3. You're going to want to stay in that room for the rest of your life. Don't. The more time you take in there, the **bigger deal** it becomes. Give yourself a minute to calm down. Then get dressed and come on out.

4. Chances are, the boy is going to be as **embarrassed** as you are—and just as interested in pretending it never happened. If he *does* crack a joke, drill a hole in him with your eyes and say, "Grow up."

using logic

Ask yourself a bunch of logical questions, and you should end up with a sensible solution.

how to calm a crying baby

1. A crying baby is trying to tell you something. Your job is to figure out what it is. **What might she want?** Try one idea after another till you find something that works. Start with a little comforting. Talk to her. Sing a little song. If she lost her pacifier or her toy penguin, give it back.

2. That didn't work? O.K., then. **Pick her up.** Hold her on your shoulder. Walk around the room or rock her gently in a chair. Babies love rhythmic movements.

3. Pat her softly on the back. If she's got **air** in her stomach, this will help her burp.

4. Sometimes a baby's just **bored.** Turn on the mobile. Show her that polka-dot bunny. Offer her an interesting baby toy to hold. Take her to a mirror so she can look at her face.

5. Other times a baby's **tired and overstimulated.** If you've been playing with her for a long time, try calming things down. She might need a nap.

6. Think: Is there anything that could be **bothering her?** Might she have a dirty diaper? Better check. Maybe the stereo's too loud. Maybe the desk light is shining in her eyes. Maybe she's too hot in that fuzzy jumpsuit, or too cold without it.

7. Hungry? Could be. Try giving her a bottle.

8. If the baby keeps on crying, you may feel upset inside. Don't show it—not one little bit. Keep being gentle in all you do. **Never yell** at a baby, and never, ever shake one.

9. Sometimes **parents will tell you** that a baby is hurting because she's getting new teeth or has a sore bottom. If so, they may also tell you what to do about it. Follow any instructions carefully. But never give a baby anything medicated— even diaper ointment—if the parent didn't O.K. it in advance.

10. If you've run out of ideas and the baby is still crying hard—**call the parents.** Get their advice.

disaster blaSter

Ask the parents to tell you about the baby's habits before they leave. Does the baby fuss for an hour every evening before she goes to bed? Does she have any special bedtime rituals? Maybe she likes the yellow rattle better than the red one. Maybe she likes it when a babysitter sings "Jingle Bells" in a chipmunk voice. Find out. Then, if she gets crabby, you'll know what to try.

Come back, Shane!

how to find a lost dog

1. Where might he **go?** If he always heads for a certain place when you go on walks, check there. Go slow as you look. Call your dog's name. Listen.

2. What **sounds** make your dog come? Shaking the biscuit box? The Tweety bird squeak toy? Whatever makes that sound, take it with you on the hunt.

3. How can you cover more ground? By **calling friends.** Get a search party going. Divide up the neighborhood. Search in pairs on foot, on bikes, and in cars. Call neighbors. Let them know your dog's missing so that they can be on the lookout, too.

4. Where might someone who found a lost dog take him? The **Humane Society.** So go over and see if he's there. (You can call, but it's safer to check yourself.) Visit again a few days later. Talk to local veterinarians, too.

5. Throw the net wider yet. Make **flyers** to post around the neighborhood. The flyers should include:

the date your dog got lost,
the dog's name,
a description,
a photograph,
and your phone number.

Do not include your name. If someone calls and says they've found your pet, have your parents ask some careful questions. Every now and then, a person will pretend to have a pet to get a reward or a fee. Don't be so excited that you let your guard down.

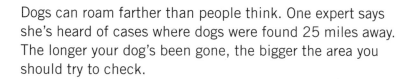

6. Think big. Put a "dog lost" ad in the local **newspaper** (many times such ads are free). Check the "pet found" ads, too.

Dogs can roam farther than people think. One expert says she's heard of cases where dogs were found 25 miles away. The longer your dog's been gone, the bigger the area you should try to check.

7. If your dog was lost when you were in a natural area—a park, the woods, the country—he might return to the place he saw you last. Put something at that spot that **smells like you**—a sweatshirt, say. Return and check. He might be curled up in the folds, dreaming of you.

disaster blaSter

Dog tags tell the world your dog belongs to you. Be sure that your pet wears his all the time and that it includes your family's name and phone number. Your family might also want your dog to get a microchip—a tiny ID chip that your vet puts under the animal's skin that can be read by special scanners. With a microchip, your dog can be identified even if he has lost his collar.

if your ride doesn't show ∧

1. Is there anyone around you **know and trust?** If so, don't hesitate to flag her down before she drives away. Tell her your situation. You don't want to be left alone if you can help it.

2. Usually, these kinds of situations are a result of some mix-up. Once the adults realize what's happened, they'll come and get you. Where will they come? Here. So if you are left alone, **stay put.** You want to be someplace where they can find you, not a half mile away trying to walk home.

3. If you've waited a half hour and there's still no sign of your ride, it's time to find a **phone.** If you're in a place where phones are hard to come by—a soccer field, say—go to a nearby store, gas station, or restaurant. Call another relative, your best friend's mom, or a trusted neighbor.

4. Then again, say there are no businesses nearby. If an hour has passed and you have absolutely no other option, ring a doorbell at a nearby house. In some towns, the police have special signs that get posted in the windows of houses they think are **safe for kids.** Look for one of those houses first. If there aren't any, the house with the kids' toys in the yard might be a good choice. Ask someone there to call for you. They may ask you in—it's the nice thing to do. Say no, thanks, and stay on the porch. It's safer. If these people can't get your parents or some other adult you know well, have them call the police. The police can come drive you home.

disaster bla**S**ter

**Talk with your parents about what to do if you should get stranded.
Carry important phone numbers with you and know how to call collect.
Most important: take an extra minute or two when you're going out the door
to be sure everybody's clear on when you need to be picked up,
who's going to do it, and where to meet.**

if you get on the wrong bus

1. Should you get off? Ix-nay. You're better off sitting on a bus than wandering around a neighborhood you don't know. **Stay where you are** till you have a plan.

2. Who can help? **The driver.** Tell him where you need to go. He may tell you to stay on this bus because it will circle back eventually to the place you got on. He can also call the bus company or the police to send help.

3. Even more likely, the driver may give you a flyer and explain how you can **transfer** to a different bus that will take you home. If that's the case, write down the name or number of the bus you need to transfer to. Double-check the route with the second driver when you get on.

4. If there's no good way to transfer, and this bus stops at a store or a **mall you know,** you could get off and call your parents from there.

5. And, of course, never let a stranger from the bus—even the driver—walk or take you home. But **you knew that,** righ

keeping cool in scary situations

If you keep your mind on
what to do (not how you feel),
you think better.

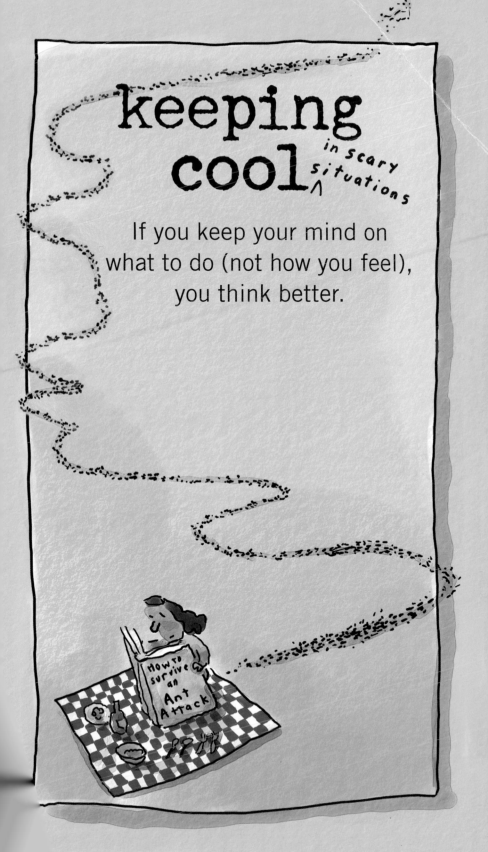

how to stay safe in a storm

1. Dark clouds are piling up, and you hear a roll of thunder. Do you really want to keep playing till it starts raining? No. Anytime there's thunder, there can be lightning. Go in now. **Don't wait** for the storm to hit.

2. How can you **prepare?** Close the doors and windows. Get a flashlight in case the lights go off. Turn on the radio or TV to a local channel or check the cable weather channel. Look and listen for information that pertains to your town and county.

3. If you hear **SEVERE THUNDERSTORM WATCH,** weather conditions in your area are right for severe thunderstorms.

If you hear **SEVERE THUNDERSTORM WARNING,** a storm will hit soon.

Thunderstorms may bring strong, damaging winds and lots of rain, as well as thunder and lightning. To find out how far away from you the storm is, count how many seconds pass between the time you see lightning and the time you hear thunder. Then divide that number by five. For instance, say you count to 10. $10 \div 5 = 2$. So the storm is about two miles away.

Lightning

Lightning is a big charge of electricity. It can hurt a person—even kill him. Knowing a few things can help you stay safe.

Lightning is attracted to metal and water; it also tends to hit things that stick up higher than the things around them. This means that, even if you're inside, you should not touch:

NO

- **phones** (except cell phones or a cordless phone removed from its base),
- **metal windows and doors,**
- **electrical cords or the things they're attached to,**
- **plumbing fixtures** (this is not the time to wash dishes or take a bath), and **fireplaces.**

These are the things that could be electrified if lightning should hit your house.

If you're stuck outside during a thunder and lightning storm because, say, you're camping, you should avoid:

NO

- **tall trees** (because they might be hit),
- **wide-open spaces** (because in a wide-open space, you become the tallest thing),
- **hilltops** (too high),
- **all water** (if you're boating, get to shore as fast as you can and wait out the storm),
- **all metal** (like golf clubs, metal fences, light poles, and backpacks with metal frames).

Instead, look for shelter under a shorter tree. Squat on the balls of your feet with your hands over your ears. Don't lie down. A car—with a hard roof and the windows rolled up—is another good place to be.

4. What will make you feel good? Not standing at the window watching the storm. **Curl up** with a snack and read a book. Play charades with your sisters. Keep the TV tuned to weather information. If the lights go off, use your flashlight. Workers are probably already on the way to repair the line. Tell yourself that.

5. A heavy rain may leave **water in your basement** or pouring down your street. Avoid both. That water in the street is more powerful than it looks—maybe powerful enough to sweep a person down a storm sewer. And inside or out, the water could be electrified—and contain sewage. (Yick.) Stay on the sofa. Have a glass of milk. Enjoy feeling comfy.

Tornadoes

If you're watching TV or listening to the radio

and you hear

TORNADO WATCH,

weather conditions are good for tornadoes.

If you hear

TORNADO WARNING,

a tornado has been spotted somewhere in the area.

A tornado warning does NOT mean a tornado is coming down your street. But if you hear a warning, go to the basement, just to be safe. If there is no basement, go to the lowest floor of the building and find an enclosed place (like a closet or a bathroom) away from windows and doors.

If you're outside, spot a tornado, and can't get to a building, look for a low area—a ditch or the bottom of a hill. Lie down and put your hands on your head.

if you're caught in a rip current

1. If you're swimming in the ocean and you feel yourself being pulled out to sea, you may be caught in a rip current. A rip current is a **strong flow of water** going away from the beach.

Even a good adult swimmer can get caught by a rip current.

2. Don't fight the current by trying to swim straight for shore against it.

3. Instead, **swim parallel to the shore** until you feel the current relax. Once it quits pulling on you, turn and head for land.

4. What if the current is so strong that you can't even swim parallel? **Tread water or float.** Let the water carry you so you don't get tired out. Yell and wave so others know you're in trouble. Either someone will come out and get you or eventually the current will weaken and let you free.

disaster blaSter

- Never swim on a beach without a lifeguard.

- Before you get your toes wet, ask the lifeguard where the safest places are to swim on that beach.

- Check out the water yourself. Sometimes rip currents are completely invisible to the eye, but other times you can spot one as a muddy-looking river flowing away from land or a choppy, foamy surface on the water.

- Take a buddy with you when you go in the water. If one of you gets into trouble, the other can go for help. Make sure an adult is watching you from shore, too.

- Avoid swimming near rock jetties, reefs, and piers. They can create rip currents.

- Don't swim when the water's rough—the bigger the waves, the stronger the rip currents. Even on calm days, don't swim straight out to sea as if you're headed for Tahiti. Stick near the shore. If you want to practice your butterfly, do so parallel to the beach.

if you fall through the ice

1. Yell—loud—to let people know you need help. Then face the direction you came from. That's where the ice is probably strongest. Put your arms on the ice and **kick as hard as you can** to lift yourself back up out of the water.

2. If you're able to get out, **don't stand up.** Stay on your stomach and wiggle back the way you came.

3. If you're not able to get out, hold onto the edge and bring your knees up to your chest. It will **conserve your body heat** until help comes. Your clothes may feel heavy, but don't take them off. Even wet, they help keep you warmer, and the danger of this situation lies in getting so cold that you can't move.

4. If you're on the ice with a friend, tell her to get on her stomach (that will distribute her weight) and not to come near the hole. If she did, she might fall through, too, and there'd be nobody to rescue either one of you. Instead, she should slither away to firm ground and **get an adult to help.**

If there is absolutely nobody else around? Your friend can lie on firm ice or solid ground and throw you one end of something long and skinny—a rope, a long stick, a scarf. As she holds one end, you grab the other and hoist yourself out.

if you're in an earthquake

1. Get **away from windows,** mirrors, and anything else made of glass that could break and cut you. Get away from anything that might topple over on you, too—bookshelves that aren't attached to the wall, cupboards with doors that don't latch, and so on.

2. Look for a **big, solid object** in the room—say, a sturdy table or desk against an inside wall. Get under the table, hold onto one of the legs, and protect your eyes by pressing your face against your arm.

3. If you're in bed when the earthquake hits, get **under the bed** and stay there, curled up. Cover your head with a pillow.

4. If you live in an apartment building, expect the **fire alarm** and the sprinklers to go off.

5. If you're outdoors, keep away from **power lines.**

6. When the house stops shaking, stay where you are and call out so your parents know where to find you. If you're alone and you **smell gas,** get out of the place immediately. The fires that sometimes follow an earthquake can be a bigger problem than the quake itself. Go to a neighbor's and call 911.

7. After an earthquake, there is often a smaller, second series of shakes called an **aftershock.** Expect it. Stay near a safe spot. (Talk to your parents now—before anything happens—about just where in your home those spots may be.)

if you're separated from your parents in the city

1. Don't go looking for them. Unless there's something unsafe about it, **stay** as close as you can to the place you saw them last. That's where they're likely to look for you.

2. **Tell an adult** what's happened. If you're in a big stadium, go to a security guard. If you're on the street, try to find a police officer or go into a public business (like a store or a restaurant). In a store or mall, a clerk may be able to page your parents. Failing that, an adult can always call the police.

3. Wait in a **public place** while the adult goes to work on your problem. Do not go into a back room or someone's car (unless it's a police car) or any other place removed from other people. It's safer to be with a lot of different people than to be alone with one.

4. **Leave a message for your parents** any way you can—via cell phone or pager or answering machine. If you're on vacation, that means calling the place you're staying. Your parents can call there, too, and get the information.

disaster blaSter

- When you're traveling, be sure you know the name of your hotel or the people with whom you're staying. Write the name and phone number on a piece of paper and stick it in your pocket. Take coins for a public phone. A little extra money might be helpful, too.

hotel McHuge
555-5678

- Pay attention—don't follow your parents around in a fog. When your mom checks the subway map, look at it, too. When you enter a huge mall, notice things that mark the door you came in by. It helps to have a sense of where you are and where you've been.

- Finally, talk about these things with your mom and dad. Have a family plan. It will be easier to find one another if everybody knows what to expect.

if you're lost from the group on a hike

1. **Stay put.** There are going to be people looking for you, and you don't want to wander off in the opposite direction by mistake. That said, if there's an open area nearby, go there. You'll be easier to spot than if you huddle under a tree.

2. **Make noise.** Hoot. Holler. Do what you can to let searchers know where you are.

3. Don't let yourself get **cold.** If you've got a jacket, zip it up. If you've got a hat, wear it. If it gets dark—O.K., this is scary, but you can handle it: Gather some tree limbs or brush or dried leaves. Make a bed so you're not lying on cold, bare ground. Put some of that brush on top of you, and you'll have a kind of blanket as well.

4. It's morning? Crow like a rooster. **Help the folks** who've been out there beating the bush for you all night find you in time for a big waffle-and-bacon breakfast.

disaster blaSter

Carry a few basic supplies in your pack when you're going on a hike: a bottle of water, a pack of matches, a baggie of trail mix, and a garbage bag (instant raincoat). Throw in a whistle, too. (All the better to hear you with, my dear.) Should you somehow end up alone, your stay in the woods will be more pleasant, and shorter, too.

being
strong

Meet your problems head on.
You'll find out you're
stronger than you think.

if you flunk a test

1. Your first thought may be, →

> I'm going to have to drop out of school and pull dandelions for a living since I'm so STUPID.

But you're not. Flunking means you didn't understand the material. You can **fix** that.

2. The second thought may be, →

> I'm going to flunk this course.

No. Not on the basis of **one test** you won't.

3. Third thought: →

> I think I'll tear this up into atoms.

Not a good idea. For one thing, your parents will find out anyway—guaranteed. For another, you need to **look the test over** to see what you missed.

4. Ask your teacher to sit down with you before or after school and go over **what you missed.** Make a list of the things you don't understand.

5. Get somebody to work with you on that material at home: your parents, your big brother, the teenager next door. Give the subject some **extra time** each day. The work's not going to get easy in one day or two, but give it a month and you'll be understanding more and doing better.

if a friend wants to copy
your homework

1. You know it **isn't fair** for her to get credit for work you did. Say so. Take a deep breath and say no.

2. Offer to **help her study** if she's having trouble with the material.

3. Your friend may be

frustrated
(by not getting what she wants),

scared
(of a bad grade),

scared

and ashamed
(because she knows she's in the wrong).

ashamed

All these things may **make her mad.** Let her feel that way. Be nice and calm but stick to your guns. If she keeps it up, say, "I'm not going to argue with you about this. I'm going now. See you tomorrow." If she's any kind of friend, she'll behave better when you see her next. And she won't ask you to do this sort of thing again.

if you don't make the team

1. **Talk** to your mom or dad. Let them comfort you. They'll probably remind you how tough the competition was and list all the things you do especially well. You know it all already, but it will feel good to hear it again.

2. Talk to **another girl** who didn't get picked. Ask how she feels and what she plans to do instead. Tell her how you feel, too.

3. It might be tough, but talk to **the coach** about what you can do to make the team next time. It helps to know exactly what you need to work on.

4. Let the hurt settle for a couple of days while you **think** about what to do next. Is there another sport you like? Try it. If not, then . . .

5. Don't let one tryout stand between you and the game you love. If you didn't make (say) the premier soccer team, look for a soccer team in a slightly **less competitive** league. Before you join, go to a practice to see if you like the coach and other girls.

6. Look good? Sign up. **Work on your skills.** Make some new friends. You'll be a better player at the end of the year. At that point you can try out again for that first team— unless, of course, it turns out you like the one you're on so much, you want to stay where you are.

if you get blamed for losing the game

1. **Who says** you made the team lose? The same girl who blamed somebody else last week? Who's she to judge? She may be the best player on the team, but that doesn't give her the right to dump on you or anybody else. Tune her out. Other girls will, too.

2. O.K. So you made a mistake. But what about the mistake **somebody else** made five minutes before yours that cost you guys a goal? And the mistake back in the first half that allowed one? Your team's position at the end of the contest is the result of **many, many moves** by everybody on both teams. Rarely is it fair to say that one player cost a win.

3. You're not perfect. **Don't beat yourself up** about it. Sometimes we can be our own worst critics. Figure out why things went wrong so they won't happen again. Then move on. Treat yourself the way you would treat someone else in your shoes.

4. Give credit where credit's due. Maybe your team didn't so much lose this game as the **other team won it**.

5. Of course, you may know all this and still feel bad. So get some of the disappointment off your chest. Send an e-mail to your friend who moved to Australia. Talk to your big sister. Call another best friend. Write in your diary. Put your **feelings into words.** You'll feel lighter.

6. Make something **fun** happen. Challenge your brother to a game of Boggle. Teach the little girl next door how to stand on her head. Ask your mom if she'll teach you to bake biscuits. If you aren't ready for company, curl up with your favorite book. Turn on your favorite CD. Tell yourself that time's going to take care of this, because it will.

if you're threatened by a bully

1. People who push other people around like to have **victims.** That doesn't mean you have to be one. Let this bully know you can't be pushed. Face him down. Tell him exactly what he's doing and why he should stop:

2. Tell him what you want him to do:

3. If the bully is a friend who's taking advantage of you, let him know that you're still ready to be friends **if he quits** acting this way.

4. Of course, there are **scarier** kinds of bullies: Older kids who say and do things designed to upset you. Boys who do the same with sexual talk. Kids who you think may hurt you physically.

If you're dealing with a bully like this and he (or she) does not leave you alone when you tell him to, then you need to **get help.** Tell your parents. Talk to your teacher and the principal at school. Somebody has to talk to the kid's parents as well. He should know that he's got one option, and one only: to lay off.

1. Lying. Cheating. Stealing. A girl who knows she's guilty may be frozen with shame and fear at such words. If that girl is you, **be brave.** Admit what you did. Not only is this the right thing to do, it is also the smartest. You've seen what happens to people when they try to cover things up. The mess goes on and on, and the shame gets worse. Get it over with. Cut your losses. Tell the truth.

2. Accept responsibility. You've heard other people make **lame excuses** for themselves. Did you admire it? Didn't think so. Treat yourself with more respect.

3. Apologize. It makes a difference.

4. Ask what you can do to **help make things right**—or at least as right as they can be. Then do it.

5. Accept the **punishment.** Hard? Sure. But show honor in these things, and you'll come out of this with something to feel good about.

if you're wrongly accused

1. Try not to get mad. **You know** you didn't do it. Keep your mind on that, not on the anger and excitement of others. Breathe deeply. Talk slowly. Don't yell.

2. Tell the truth in a calm voice.

3. Tell the truth in a calm voice.

4. Tell the truth in a calm voice.

5. If they still don't believe you and you're going to be punished? It's out of your hands. You have to accept it. Know that **the truth is going to come out** in time, and when it does, you can look back at your own behavior with pride, and others can do so with admiration.

things they never taught you in school

There are tricks for solving all sorts of problems.

if you spill cherry soda on the carpet

1. Wet spills are easier to clean up than dry ones, so be quick. Get a white paper towel (or a clean cloth) and press it onto the spill. **Don't rub or scrub.** As the soda gets soaked up, find other dry places on the towel and keep blotting. Work from the outside of the spill into the center.

2. When all the spill is absorbed, put a cup of water in a bowl with a little liquid laundry **soap**—a quarter teaspoon should do it. Put some of this soapy water on a second, clean paper towel. Give the towel a good squeeze, then blot the carpet again.

3. Spray or **sprinkle** clean water over the spot. (Not too much. You want the carpet wet but not soaking.) Blot it up with dry paper towels.

4. Cover the spot with yet more dry paper towels. Put something heavy on it—say, a nice, fat phone book—and **leave it** overnight. The paper towels should suck up the rest of the soda.

5. In the morning, pick up the phone book so that the carpet can **dry.** Is there still a mark? Then mix a half teaspoon of white vinegar into two-thirds of a cup of water. With a parent's help, test the mixture on a small, out-of-the-way bit of carpet. If it doesn't hurt that carpet, use it to blot the spot as you did before. Again, just be sure your mom or dad is there to supervise.

other stains on washable fabrics

blood on your pants
Soak the pants for an hour in a bucket of cool water to remove the worst of the stain. Then stick them in the wash as you usually do. (If you can't do laundry right away, let the pants dry before putting them in the hamper.)

chocolate on your big sister's T-shirt
Let the chocolate dry, then scrape it off with a dull butter knife. Now the shirt's ready for a warm, soapy wash.

mushed raspberries on your aunt's white tablecloth
Carefully pick the berry bits off the cloth. Soak the cloth in cool water, then wash it in warm water.

french-fry grease on the sofa
Dust the spot with talcum powder. Let the powder sit for 10 minutes, absorbing the grease. Then vacuum it off.

chewing gum on your friend's mitten
Put the mitten in a plastic bag and put it in the freezer. When the gum gets hard, it should break or lift right off. Wash the mittens as soon as possible.

ink on your sleeve
Blot the spot with denatured alcohol. (Check the label on the bottle.) Ask your mom to launder the shirt as usual with bleach. And if the pen said "permanent"? It probably is.

if a mean dog chases you

1. A short lesson in dog language:

screaming + running = "Come and get me."

All dogs are chasers.

They chase balls.

They chase sticks.

And, friendly or unfriendly, if you run, they will chase you.

So the first thing to do if a dog comes toward you in an angry way is to stop and stand still. You can turn to the side, but don't turn around.

2. Keep your hands down. Don't talk to the dog or look him in the eye. Most dogs who come at you barking aren't mean; they're scared. **Avoiding his eyes** will make you seem less threatening.

3. Your average dog will bark for a while and then lose interest. At that point, you can begin to **back slowly away.** You can sidestep, but, again, don't turn your back to the dog.

4. If the dog lunges for you, give him **something else to bite**—your purse or your backpack, your bike or your jacket. Put anything you can between you and the dog, and do everything you can to stay on your feet. Don't worry about things getting ripped. You come first.

disaster blaSter

Don't try to make friends with strange dogs. You don't know them, and they don't know you. Even if you're going into a friend's house for the first time and she tells you her dog is friendly, you should be a little cautious.

Give a dog a chance to see and sniff you before you try to touch him. If he seems relaxed—if he's moving freely and is not tense or stiff— pet him on the side of the face, under his ears, or under his chin. Do not pet him on top of his head or get down and hug him. Both things can be threatening to a dog, and this one may not be sure whether he can trust you.

if you're asked to dance,

and want to but don't know how

1. The secret to dancing is that **there's no secret.** People simply listen to the music and make it up. It's not as if you have to fake it. All you need to do is stand up.

2. Listen to the music. Hear the beat? Start tapping your toes. Once you get that rhythm, start moving the rest of you, too.

tap
tap

3. Watch other kids. What are they doing? Do the same thing.

4. Sometimes having a **picture in your mind** can be an inspiration. Hop up and down like popcorn. Pretend you're holding on to an invisible steering wheel. Or wave your arms back and forth like windshield wipers.

5. Get loose.
Be happy.

how not to fall off a horse

1. If your horse tries to run away with you, stay calm.
Sit back in the saddle—think of it as sitting on your back
pockets. Don't lean forward. If the horse veers, you might
keep going over the top of his head.

2. Grip with your thighs and keep your lower legs relaxed.
Try not to let your legs flop around or nudge the horse with
your calves. He will think you want him to go faster.

3. Shorten one side of the reins, using your other hand to
keep a strong grip on the leather as you slide the first hand
forward. Let the short-rein hand sit on your thigh and **pull
the horse into a turn.** The horse will have to slow down. Keep
pulling, forcing him in smaller and smaller circles until he
stops. You'll have more power if you keep your arms close
to your body.

4. If you've lost a stirrup, don't lean over. Let your **toes be
smart** and find it.

5. If you need more stability, grab onto **the saddle.** On an English saddle, there is often a little strip of leather called a bucking strap. On a Western saddle, grab the pommel. You can also hold onto the horse's mane at the withers—the little crest at the base of his mane. It won't hurt the horse.

6. If you lose the reins, sit back, hold on, and wait for your horse to come to a stop. Whatever he's got in mind—whether he's headed for the barn or wants to go to the side of the ring to sniff noses with a friend—he's not going to keep going **forever.** Just concentrate on keeping your seat, and you'll be all right.

disaster blaSter

Lots of times, horses on a trail ride will begin to go faster on the way back because they want to get to the barn. Be prepared. Stay in the middle of the line, not at the front, so the horses ahead of you set the pace. Remind your horse you're there by talking to him and patting him on the withers.

If your horse starts picking up speed, give him something else to think about by turning his head a little to the right for two steps, then to the left for two steps; then the right, then the left; and so on. Turn him in a circle if you have to. It's a way of saying, "We're going to get there when I want to, pal, so you may as well relax."

if you're bugged, by a bee

or stung!

1. Don't take swings in the air when a bee flies by to check you out. Move s-l-o-w-l-y. You are much, *much,* **much** more likely to get stung if the bee gets nervous than if it doesn't.

2. Get rid of things that might be attracting the bee. **Cover your food.** Bees love soft drinks, so put a top on your drink or peek inside the can before taking a sip. (You do *not* want to get stung in the mouth.) Finish the drink inside if you have to. Take simple precautions. If your backyard is full of clover, put your shoes on.

3. What if the bee gets you anyway? Well, if there's a stinger in your skin, don't pull it out with your fingers. Instead, **scrape it out** with one quick movement using something with an edge—say, your school ID card. Squeezing the stinger could release more venom into your skin. Tell an adult you've been stung so that he or she can help.

4. The spot where you were stung is going to sting and itch for a while. Wash the area, but **don't rub** or scratch it. That will only spread the venom. Don't be surprised if the spot gets red, swells, or develops a small bump—that's normal.

5. Wrap some **ice** in a dish towel. Hold it to your skin. If you were stung in the mouth, suck some ice or eat a Popsicle.

6. Rest. A lot of running around will get your blood moving and spread the hurt.

7. Be on the lookout for an **allergic reaction.** Tell an adult right away if your chest feels tight, your tongue is swelling, or you feel a little dizzy. If you're home alone, call 911. An allergic reaction can be dangerous, so take it seriously.

disaster blaSter

Wear light-colored clothes during bee season. Believe it or not, bees like dark colors and floral prints. They like perfumey things, too. Lay on the raspberry body splash, the lilac bath powder, or the scented hair gel, and to a bee you'll seem as inviting as a flower bed. Keep the scents on the shelf until the weather changes.

if you need a bra and don't know how to buy one

1. When you look at a bunch of bras in a store, you'll see they have **sizes** like 32A and 34B.

The number tells a shopper how big the band of the bra is when it's fastened.

The letter tells how big the cup is that goes around the breast.

2. To find out your size, you'll need a measuring tape. If you don't have one at home, that's O.K. They'll have one at the store.

First measure around **your chest,** just below your breasts. (You can keep your shirt on as long as it's not bulky.) If you get an even number, add four inches to get your number size. If you get an odd number, add five inches. (For instance, if you measure 32, your number size is probably 36, since 32 plus 4 is 36. If the tape says 29, your number size is probably 34, since 29 plus 5 is 34.)

3. Now figure out your **cup size.** Measure around your chest at your nipples. If you get the same number you got when you measured below your breasts, you are probably letter size AA or AAA.
If your second number is one inch more than your first, you are probably letter size A.

        2 inches more = B   4 inches more = D
        3 inches more = C   5 inches more = DD or E

4. Once you know your number and letter size, you're ready to check out the bras. Go to a store with a **good selection** and take somebody to help—your mom or your sister or your good friend. Spend some time looking through the racks. Find two styles that look comfy, pick out several sizes, and head for the dressing room.

5. When you're trying on a bra, fasten the chest band at the loosest hook. Adjust the shoulder straps. They should be tight enough that they aren't falling off your shoulders but loose enough to feel comfortable. Stop and **really think** about how the bra fits.

The bra should be lower in the back than it is in front. If the band around your chest feels too tight, you may need a bigger number size. If the cup is baggy and loose, you may need a smaller cup size. Try on lots of different number/letter-size combinations to be sure. Ask your mom or your friend or the saleswoman to help you get what you need off the racks.

disaster blaSter

Beware of dark colors and bold patterns. That bra with the red hearts may look great on the rack, but you won't be as happy with it when hearts show up through your shirts. Go with beige or white, especially for a first bra. You want to be able to wear it with everything.

if you know you're going to look like a total geek again in your school picture

1. The night before, think about what to wear so you don't wake up and find that the shirt you want is in the wash. Go with **solid colors** and simple styles. Patterns and logos in a picture frame are like too much noise in a small room.

2. You want your hair **clean and combed** but natural. Don't start experimenting with some fancy new 'do 15 minutes before the bus comes. The chance that you'll be happy with the results is slim.

3. Makeup? You may want to cover up a pimple or two, but **don't overdo** it.

4. As you're waiting in line for the photographer, think of something that makes you truly **happy**—say, the way your baby sister smears food on her face, or the birthday party your friend threw for her dog. Put the thought in your pocket.

5. When it's your turn, march up and take a seat. **Sit up straight.** It looks 3,000 percent better than a slouch. Stretch your neck up, too, and then lower your chin a tiny bit.

6. If this is what you're going for . . .

talk and make jokes with your friends in line. Otherwise, **keep your mind** on what you're doing.

7. Look just above the lens. Tell yourself the camera is **a friend.** Then take your happy thought out of your pocket and let the smile spread over your face.

last thoughts

You've got a secret weapon
against all kinds of troubles,
and that secret weapon is **you.**

Get advice when you can.
Learn what you can.
Accept help from those who love you.
But don't look to others for all the answers.

You can stand on your own two feet.
You've got a good brain.
You've got common sense.
Keep them handy.

Trust yourself.
You'll be able to handle just about anything.